GOODBYE MY CHILD

by Margaret M. Pike
Sara Rich Wheeler

Illustrated by Shari Borum Enbody

A Centering Corporation Resource
ISBN# 1-56123-052-9

D1445130

Additional copies may be ordered from: Centering Corporation
1531 N Saddle Creek Rd
Omaha NE 68104-5064
(402) 553-1200

A Mother's Story

Jeanne White, Mother of Ryan White

From the time my son, Ryan, was diagnosed with AIDS in 1984 until he died at age 18 in 1990, we received more than 60,000 cards. Because of the media attention he received, flowers came from all over the country to the hospital and to our home.

As much as we had the support of a nation and the world, I was like any other grieving parent after he died. I had no idea what to do - how to plan his funeral, how to grieve, how to go on.

We had to find our own way. It was hard at times, with many people telling us how to live and how to believe. We had people tell us that Ryan would have lived if he believed more strongly, or that he would not have gotten AIDS had he gone to their church. These comments were very hurtful as I struggled with my own feelings of faith.

Despite all the mail we received, no one gave me materials about grieving or about planning a funeral. Certainly, there were inspirational materials sent in those many letters, but nowhere was there a book like this.

I knew Ryan had AIDS for five and a half years before he died, yet I never prepared for his funeral because I didn't want to plan on Ryan's death. But Ryan had plans. He picked out the place where he wanted to be buried and what he would wear, even down to his underwear. He wanted to be buried in his Guess Jeans, Town and Country shirt, sun glasses and boxer underwear.

When he told me about the boxer underwear, I laughed. He had a hernia that prevented his wearing jockey briefs. He was thinking about his comfort later on.

If it weren't for our friend, Elton John, I would have been at a total loss about how to plan Ryan's funeral. Elton had never been through a loss of this type, yet he helped us plan the funeral. Elton wanted the biggest and best for Ryan's casket, but respected my decisions. I chose a modest casket of wood that I am convinced Ryan would prefer.

We had photos of Ryan everywhere in church - baby photos, high school photos and photos with celebrities. We also had other memorabilia that told of his earlier years, such as toys like G.I.Joe. Ryan would have liked that.

We also put his plastic Guardian Angel night light in his casket. This light, a gift from a good friend of the family and member of our church, went with him to every hospitalization. We turned it on at home each night. As we closed his casket at the funeral, I turned it off and took it out. It was inspirational for him and continues to be for us. We still turn the light on for weekends and on holidays.

I especially appreciate how this book deals with siblings. From the beginning, Ryan had medical problems relating to hemophilia. I knew my daughter, Andrea, needed attention and I tried to give it to her during those years before he developed AIDS from the blood components used to treat his bleeding disorder. But when Ryan was sick and in the hospital, I was with him. He was the one who received the media attention, not Andrea.

She felt jealous when he received so much media attention. She never thought anything would happen to him. It was not until he died that she really understood.

After Ryan died, she had a terrible time and didn't want to come home because he would not be there. Finally, one night I convinced her to talk about it. "AIDS took my brother's life. We don't have it anymore." She told me. "We lived with AIDS for five and a half years, every day of our lives. I don't care to ever hear that word again."

Because of that important conversation, I was surprised to learn several months later that she had changed her career plans. Instead of wanting to be an air traffic controller, she plans to become a doctor caring for children with infectious diseases.

In my mind, Ryan received so much attention because he gave hope to the hopeless. I don't think it was just because he had AIDS.

He liked to talk to kids about AIDS because he felt they would listen and this would be their disease. He knew that when adolescents experiment with drugs and sex they put themselves at risk.

Today, I talk to high school and college students about AIDS. We have the Ryan White fund, an educational program in Los Angeles and Indiana, to help children with infectious diseases. I know I am lucky being able to talk about Ryan. Not many parents have that opportunity. Too few friends and relatives bring up the name of a child who has died for fear it will make the grieving parents sad. In reality, the silence is much more difficult.

After Ryan's death, I had a need to do something with my energy and time which had been centered on his care. I felt like I could conquer the world. I also wanted to keep busy so I wouldn't have time to think about anything else, especially the loss of my son.

I think my mourning process has been slow, but I was helped because Ryan's last week was so horrible. He had severe bleeding in his brain and was on a kidney dialysis machine. I knew that Ryan would never want to survive if he would be forever in that condition. It would have been selfish of me to have him *not* die just to have him.

He was given medicine once to start his heart after it stopped. I had no idea that I could say, *No more*, but it was time to stop prolonging his inevitable death. After much thought I told Ryan, *It's OK. It's OK to let go.* I know he was hanging on for me.

I continue to visit Ryan's grave and find I enjoy meeting other bereaved parents. We each decorate our children's grave at special times.

Like these other parents, I have an emptiness that will never be filled again. Yet I go on as they do. Our children would have wanted it that way

That is why *Goodbye My Child* is so important. I see this book as a guidepost to death and grief, yet I don't mean it in a morbid way. It takes you through the decisions that need to be made and through the thoughts and feelings you may have. It helps you find and accept your own way of thinking and feeling as OK. I hope this books helps you as it has helped me - to understand death and to appreciate life.

Jeanne

Goodbye My Child

As much as you loved your child, you probably didn't realize how much you lost until she died. Gone, are the most cherished moments in life: birthdays, Christmas, confirmation, bar or bat mitzvah, graduation, and marriage. Gone are the warm hugs, the hot arguments, the sweet smells.

Now there is a gaping wound in your heart, an unfilled place at the table, and you no longer get the spontaneous special chats as you prepare dinner. Gone, too, is a child to comfort you as you grow older.

It has been said that when your parents die, you lose your past. If your spouse dies, you lose your present. When your child dies, you lose a part of your future. All of us experience losses in life, be it our parents, spouse, siblings or our own children. When a child dies before his parents, it goes against the natural order. When that order is trampled on, it makes the world seem a little less sure and a little less safe.

It doesn't matter if your child was the tiniest infant or one who grew to adulthood and even old age. It is the *relationship* with your child that forms these powerful emotions, not the age. While the circumstances of every death are different, there are common threads in the way all parents feel when they lose a child.

So many people say I was lucky I never knew my baby. But I did.
He was very real to me and the pain is very deep.

It is so difficult to believe that I could spend six years
with my daughter and the next moment she is gone.
How does someone live through pain like that?

I loved my son as much when he was 65 as when he was three.
He was still my son and his dying before me is just unbearable.

The death of a child also has a huge effect on other children in the family. Some may be too young to understand what has happened. Grandparents may be very disturbed about a grandchild dying before them.

When Elizabeth died it felt like someone crammed their fist
down my throat and ripped out my heart.

Grieving is the process where you pick up the pieces of your shattered life and heal. It is one of the most difficult jobs you'll ever have. It is a journey without a path. Along the way you will have stops and starts, ups and downs and many turns. We all grieve differently and with individual timetables.

At times you may feel you are going crazy or that you will never feel good again. These powerful and unexpected thoughts and feelings may stay with you for months and years to come. There are many, many others who have had these same powerful emotions. You are not alone.

It's been 10 years. The pain is still there but at least now I can see her face as it was before the respirators, tubes and machines. I still think of her every day but they are happy thoughts and memories.

I thought, at times, it would be easier if I died, too.
I started to consider ways by which I could join him.
I never shared these thoughts with my husband or in the support group.
I finally told my best friend
who immediately supported me in seeking professional counseling.
The counseling helped me work though my feelings and depression.

There are no rights or wrongs to how you feel, but acting on some emotions can be very harmful. Feelings are feelings and thoughts are thoughts. Accept them as part of your recovery, but get help if you are thinking of doing something harmful to yourself or others.

What You May Need to Think About

Unfinished Business

When a child dies- -or any loved one for that matter- -there frequently are words you meant to say, love you wanted to express, a promise you intended to keep and things you wanted to do.

If you had time before the death, you may have been able to share your feelings and do something special you knew your child would like.

I remember I went over and lifted her head
and cradled her in my arms and said what I guess mothers have said
from the beginning of time: how I loved her, how fortunate I was that we
had her, and someday, we would meet again.

I embraced her when she died and kissed her warm lips, cheeks
and eyes and bathed her face with my tears. She was gone and I felt like I
had died, too. I asked God, "Why her and not me?"

In the case of sudden death, you may not have had the opportunity to say or do some things you wish you had. Unfinished business can keep families from resolving their grief and moving on. Finishing your business can help you heal.

When the doctor called and said Susie had died, I asked,
"What can we do for her now?"

You may find it helpful to:

1) Keep a promise you made to a child even if he cannot be there to see it.

2) Share your thoughts, feelings and memories with your child even if she cannot hear them. You can speak to her at her graveside or in the comfort of your home.

3) Write your thoughts and concerns in a journal or record them on a tape.

4) Write a letter to your child. Put it in the casket or keep it in a special box.

5) If you cannot speak to your child, you can express your thoughts to a caring witness.

I wrote a letter to my daughter and had it printed in the newspaper.
After reading it many times I can read it now without crying.

Organon Donation

One of the most difficult questions you may already have faced is whether to donate your child's organs. Some states require hospital staff to ask this question, which may come just before or just after death because time is critical to keep the organs in good shape so they can be given to someone.

Depending upon the cause of death of your child, body organs may or may not be able to be transplanted. Eyes nearly always can be used, but there are other requirements for organs like the kidneys, heart and lungs. Hospital staff will answer your questions.

When organs are removed, know that your child's body is treated with dignity and respect. While some parents feel their child can keep on living in a small way if the heart or kidneys are used again, others feel their child has gone through enough. Whether you donate your child's organs is a personal decision and is respected by hospital staff. It's for *you* to decide.

I was ashamed of myself after we were approached about organ donation.
I hadn't even thought about this.

He was an ideal son. When I lost him, I lost everything.
I figured this way he'd still be alive to me.
I know that he's out there somewhere, helping people.

There is an article in *People* magazine about Marva Odister, who donated all major organs of her son, Valdies Doss, after a truck/pedestrian accident took his life. Mrs. Odister explained to a hospital worker: *I'd like to spread him around.*

Autopsy

Another difficult decision is whether to permit an autopsy, an examination of the body after death. This decision comes at a time when you are in great pain, confused and upset. You may never have had to make this kind of decision before.

An autopsy is done by a pathologist, a doctor who studies body tissues to make diagnoses of disease and cause of death. The autopsy may not give you all the answers, but may help you understand why your child died.

Another reason for doing an autopsy is to help doctors learn something that could prevent a similar death in the future. Most hospitals routinely ask family members about having an autopsy performed.

Sometimes the choice about an autopsy is not up to you. An autopsy may be mandatory if your child:
1) Died during surgery or while under general anesthesia
2) Was under age 2 and had not been hospitalized since birth
3) Died suddenly or as a result of violent death
4) As a result of illegal abortion
5) Died under suspicious, or mysterious circumstances or when your doctor could not determine the cause of death
6) Died as a result of addiction to alcohol or to any drug that may have contributed to the death
7) May have died as a result of Sudden Infant Death Syndrome.

In most cases, the choice is yours. Your doctor can answer your questions and help you decide about an autopsy.

After all your questions are answered, if you want an autopsy performed, you will need to sign a consent form. The autopsy should not delay your plans for a funeral. Early results usually are available about two days after the study. Complete results take about six weeks. Because the results likely come at a time when you are searching for answers, sitting down with the doctor to discuss the findings can be especially helpful. This information may be helpful, too, if you consider having another child.

It was one way to get some answers.
Maybe one way to help someone else.

Special Memories

You will always have your child in your heart and in your mind. However, many families say that saving special things gives them comfort.

Photos - You may want to take photos or have someone take last photos or videos of your child in the hospital or at the funeral. This is not morbid, but has the potential for giving you comfort, especially later on.

My sister took pictures at the viewing. At first it made me mad, but now I look at them from time to time. Im glad I have them.

A Lock of Hair - Some families have appreciated having a lock of their childs hair. It can be taken from the back of the neck or anywhere you like.

Footprints and/or Handprints - You can trace around your childs hands or feet or use material that sets up like plaster of Paris.

A few months before he died, a friend made a plaster of paris handprint of my little boy. It has meant so much to me that I could put my hand in my sons hand.

Weight & Length/Height - You can put this in her baby book or special memento book. You can add your own physical description.

Favorite Things - Save special clothing, blanket, stuffed animals or other mementos in a sealable bag so the smell of your child wont be lost. Some parents keep hospital identification bracelets and any other materials related to the hospital stay.

I read where that if you keep your childs coat in the closet, it will seem like they are still at home. So I left Ryans scarf and jean jacket on the coat rack by the door.

Even if you think you do not want these things now, they may be treasures in later years. You can put them away until you are ready for them.

I haven't been able to paint his room and it needs it. But his fingerprints are all over the walls from seeing how high he could jump.

You can also use a symbol of your child as a reminder of your love. You may plant a tree as a living symbol or wear jewelry or special clothing.

I try to wear pink in memory of my girl.

I always plug the meters in certain parking lots because it reminds me of when my son said people who didnt pay parking meters were stealing the spot. Its my way of saying I havent forgotten him.

Giving family and friends your child's toys can help them, too.

Planning the Funeral

You may have never had to plan a funeral before. Now, suddenly you have to plan one for your much-loved child, the last thing you ever thought you would have to do.

Thinking back on that night, there were things I wish I could have done, but having never dealt with the death of a child, I was ignorant about my rights as the parent.

How do you plan a funeral for a child, for someone who was never supposed to die before you? How do you make it fit a child? How do you get through all this?

Look at the funeral as a way of expressing your love. Imagine what your son or daughter would like. Think about what would be meaningful for you and your memories.

The funeral was a wonderful tribute to him. The music was chosen by our choir director and she chose songs for the young people who attended. The homily was all about his love of baseball. I can remember those words by heart.

One of the difficulties in planning a funeral is that you may be under pressure from family members and social customs. Ministers and funeral directors also have advice. You may want to take some advice, but **be firm about what you do and do not want.** Many options are available: services at the graveside, a church or synagogue, at home or a park. You may bury your child in the ground or in a mausoleum or cremate the remains.

People used to think that parents who lost a child could or should not be expected to make funeral arrangements. Trying to spare parents pain, a family member or friend would take over, working with a funeral director. Today, it is recognized that planning a funeral is an important part of grieving. This is the last time you will care for your child's body.

We wanted people to leave with the feeling it was a changing point in their lives and that her life had a purpose.

The funeral service can be unique, with special music, an organist, words spoken by those who knew your child best. Balloons or other special mementoes, such as toys, pictures or notes written by family, brothers, sisters, friends and classmates can also have meaning.

His request to be cremated was respected. A memorial service
was held with many of his friends making presentations about his life.
It was a beautiful service. I have a video tape of the service and music.

In planning a funeral, it is easy to take on guilt, particularly if your ideas differ from tradition or what family members suggest. Keep in mind what your child would want, what gives you comfort and what you need for your memories. This is your service.

Our son's funeral was planned by his brothers, his dad,
our priest and myself. His cousins all participated in the readings.
It was very personal and loving.

Advice from Funeral Directors

After losing a child, there are so many decisions to be made that it is impossible for you to remember them all. Look at the funeral director as a guide for you at this time. Your funeral director will help you with:
- times for the funeral and visitations
- a list of decisions that need to be made
- information for the obituary and newspaper announcements

Some newspapers have a set style for obituaries. Others allow you to include whatever you want, such as things that were special about and beloved by your child. The length determines the cost.

You will also receive estimates of costs and options. Do not feel pressured. Remember, the amount of money you spend on a funeral is not a reflection of your love for the child.

You will eventually need to bring:
-information for the death certificate, such as the child's social security number.
-clothes for your child to wear, including underclothing, shoes and socks. Consider having your child wear favorite clothing: jeans, pajamas, even cowboy boots, whatever has meaning. You have the option of bathing and dressing your child. If your child wore glasses, leave them with the funeral director. A favorite recent photograph is helpful and can be placed near the casket.

You Also Can Expect to be Asked:

1. If clergy has been called and whether there is anyone else the funeral director can contact for you
2. For a list of pallbearers
3. About any music selections, an organist or a soloist
4. Whether you have a family cemetery plot and under whose name the deed is registered. If you do not have a plot, the funeral director can tell you about the options, including cemetery, mausoleums and cremation
5. If you want jewelry or personal belongings on your child, and if you would like to keep them after the service
6. If you would like to place special things in the casket
7. If your child was a baby, do you want her placed in the casket in the infant's sleeping position.
8. If you want your child to wear personal cosmetics
9. If you have any special requests concerning the service
10. Where you would like memorial contributions to go and if you would like memorials instead of flowers
11. If your adult child was a veteran or member of a fraternal or service organization, will you want military or fraternal services. You will need his discharge papers for a military service.
12. Newspapers, radio stations where you want the obituary sent
13. If you have special requests concerning a head stone. (You may design your own.) Incidentally, do not be surprised to receive multiple telephone and even in-person calls from businesses selling markers. They routinely follow-up on obituaries.

The funeral home may have information for out-of-town guests: maps, lists of motels, and transportation schedules for planes and trains.

If your child's death was the result of homicide or suicide, the funeral director can help you understand the role police will take in investigating the death. Whatever your situation, don't be afraid to ask questions and don't be afraid to do what fits you and your child. Some funeral homes have playrooms and staff to care for children while you are talking together, making plans and during services.

Most parents have found their funeral director to be an understanding and sympathetic friend. After all, you are sharing an important event together and creating something you will remember all your life.

Grief: The Journey Begins

Word that your child died may have come by a telephone call or a knock at the door. It may have come from the alarm on a monitor as your child's heart stopped beating. It doesn't matter if the death came with a fierce suddenness or after sitting by his side week after week as he struggled to live.

When the moment of death came, anticipated or not, the blow is the same and the job of grieving begins. People who have never had a loss seem to think grief is the first reaction to death - tears, a scream, or shock. But grief is a process, a journey through more emotions than you ever thought possible.

And ... you journey alone. No two people grieve the same way at the same time.

In our society, we have a strange custom of providing tremendous support to families right after a death. Once the funeral is over, support stops. There may be one or two hangers on, but even they go away much sooner than your pain. All too soon, even well-meaning people expect you to *get on with your life*. The reality of grieving takes time, *lots of time.*

Grief is the shattering process through which you will put the pieces of your life back together. Hopefully, it will be in a way that makes sense to you and evolves into a *new normal* life.

The feeling of being normal does not come overnight. It takes time to heal. In the beginning, you will have mostly bad days. Then you will have a few good moments. As time goes by, you'll have good days and bad days. Eventually, you'll have good days with some bad times.

It takes real effort to be a survivor, to find new meaning for life and to live again. This *new normal* comes when you are ready- -often 18 months to two years, but it can take several years.

Your normal life will be different than before. You will be forever changed by your loss. Not only is this person in your life gone; you have lost your innocence. No longer can you assume bad things will never happen to you. You know you are vulnerable.

Differences in Grief

It really is impossible to compare deaths of children or the pain that follows. No one death is more tragic than another, nor is there a contest about which is worse. Each loss is its own tragedy for the living family and friends. All of you are forever changed.

Our son had AIDS. We also found out that he was homosexual.
He told us after that it was worse having us know he was homosexual
than knowing he had AIDS. His dad told him being homosexual
was unimportant to us, and he told him that he loved him.
He was special and a son that we were always proud of.

There are some differences in healing, however, depending on whether the death was sudden, after a terminal illness, chronic illness or disability.

Sudden Death

*If I had any wish for parents who must lose a child it would be that they
have 24 hours warning. I never wanted my daughter to suffer,
but I wish I had just 24 hours so I could have said goodbye,
that I loved her. Of course, if I had that 24 hours,
I would have wanted another 24 hours and then another and another.*

In a few seconds your whole life changes. Without warning, you learn your child died from an accident, a sudden illness, suicide or murder. You've had no time to prepare. Literally the child is here one moment and gone the next. Suddenly, hospital officials expect you to make decisions about things you may never have thought about before- -organ donation, an autopsy, selection of a funeral home. They expect you to know what you want to do even before you have registered the loss.

*Looking back, holding our baby in the hospital after she died
was our only time alone with her before the outside world came in on us--
doctors, coroner, funeral home, --.*

The loss of a child is like a blow to the gut. With warning, you can tighten your stomach muscles to protect yourself. When the blow comes out of nowhere, it is even more devastating because you are not ready for it. Your grief may be especially difficult because the death comes so suddenly.

So often sudden death is accidental, and that makes acceptance more difficult. You may feel anger, guilt or blame yourself or others.

Anticipated Death

*From the moment our son's leukemia was diagnosed, I began
imagining his funeral. I struggled to keep those thoughts under control.
Thinking ahead may have helped prepare me for what ultimately occurred.*

Anticipate - to Feel or Know Before Hand

If your child had a long illness (as with some cancers, cystic fibrosis or muscular dystrophy,) you may have been living with a black cloud hanging over your head for weeks, months or years. As much as you tried to have a positive attitude and hope, your mind may have been imagining the death or funeral. You may have been grieving from the moment you heard the diagnosis. Not only did you have a sick child, you also may have been grieving for a loss of your life as it had been, your dreams of your child and family.

How did learning my daughter had cystic fibrosis change our lives?
From that time on we were not the "Leave It to Beaver" family.
I felt robbed that our family couldn't have that innocence,
that normal life everyone else was having.

This anticipatory grief gives you time to absorb the reality of the coming death. You may have been able to prepare yourselves, to plan for the future and say good-bye.

As you cared for your child's physical and emotional needs, you may have had a chance to give him the special messages of love and to take care of unfinished business. You may have been able to say how much he meant to you.

All this may have come during a time of pain and suffering. The last days, weeks or months may have been an exhausting struggle every day. You, your child and your family had to cope with complicated hospital treatment or home care. You worked to keep your child comfortable

Every time your child was in the hospital, you may have known things were getting worse. Knowing your child was going to die may have helped you start grieving for your child. You may have been able to tighten your stomach muscles to prepare you for the blow of death. Still, it doesn't prevent the pain. *No one is really ready for a child of any age to die.*

Anticipatory grieving is valuable only if it is done. We cannot make the assumption that people facing the death of a child will allow that reality into their minds and hearts.

The Five Phases of Mourning

Grieving is not a simple journey with a clear path, it is a journey with many ups and downs emotionally and physically. It is a journey with many individual differences.

Before your child died, you were a person, a parent, perhaps a spouse, and a son or daughter to your own parents. You had a job, whether it was in the home, outside or both. You had friends, family, interests and outside activities.

Among other influences in your life are things such as your age, sex, personality, health, feelings about your child and your sense of independence or dependence on others. All these affect your grieving.

There is also the support you have from friends and family, your relationship with your spouse, partner and any other children. Your financial and social conditions enter into your grief. Your religion and its importance in your life play a part. Add to all that how your child died plus all the other crises that may be occurring in your life.

Sometimes life is so profoundly wrong, unfair and twisted.
But you accept it and try and get through it.

While there are individual differences, most people go through five phases of mourning:

Shock
Awareness of Loss
Conservation/Withdrawal
Healing
Renewal

Shock

Regardless of whether your child died unexpectedly or after a long illness, your first reaction was shock. You likely were stunned, confused and restless. You may have felt the whole situation was unreal. You could not believe your child died.

I knew it was coming, but still I wasn't prepared for the stillness,
that it was really over. I had no idea what to do next.

One moment we were a normal, happy family
and the next minute we were in despair.
I was simply stunned, unable to believe what I heard on the telephone.

Denial and disbelief are the way your body and mind protect itself from terrible news so you can register the information. You may be restless, feel helpless and alarmed. Shock can last for a few hours or many days.

I have no idea how I got home from the hospital after my son died.
It was like I was just walking around, going through the motions.
Somebody must have helped me.

Martha Clark, in her book, *Are You Weeping With Me, God?* says shock is a blessing, for if it weren't for shock a parent's heart would surely break.

Shock usually ends sometime after the funeral, when you are at last allowed to release your tightly controlled emotions. During shock you may have dryness of the mouth and throat, sigh, feel week and helpless and not be hungry or able to sleep. You may be centered on yourself and feel unaware of life and events around you.

Thoughts of your son or daughter may never leave your mind. You may also try to distance yourself mentally from the loss to protect yourself from the pain.

People respond to shock in many different ways. Some feel numb and unresponsive. Others scream, faint, rant and rave. Still others may act as if nothing took place. The way you respond to shock after the death of your child generally, is similar to how you reacted to other crises in your life.

When we were notified of the shooting accident, I felt a pain in my
stomach as if I had a knife in me.
That pain stayed with me for at least two months.
It never went away.

Awareness of Loss

Now that the funeral is over, the full impact of the death of your son or daughter hits you with brutal force. Friends and family have returned to their normal lives and you are left with your pain.

> *I always thought the funeral would be the worst.*
> *But afterwards I felt I was hit with a sledgehammer.*
> *Everything I saw reminded me of my daughter.*
> *Sometimes it was the littlest things and I would just fall apart.*
> *I thought I was going out of my mind.*
> *And no one was around to help.*

The reminders of your child are all over your home--his favorite toy, her special dress, the drawing he made in kindergarten, even the Mother's Day gift he gave you. All can trigger physical pain and deep emotions. Sometimes you may feel like you are going crazy or on the edge of a nervous breakdown.

What you are going through is a form of **separation anxiety,** the same emotions, intensified a hundred times, that you felt the first time you left your parents to go to school or away to camp. One of the difficulties is you likely are struggling to stay in control, an impossible task. You feel vulnerable and afraid and have numerous emotional outbursts.

> *My daughter had never been away from home for more than a month in*
> *her whole life. I think we are just plain lonesome for her*
> *after all the years she's been here with us.*

You may yearn for your child, a physical feeling as well as an emotional longing for her. You also may be searching for an answer for that unanswerable question- -**why** your child died.

> *I just looked at my husband and said, ''Is this a test, Frank?*
> *Is this what people go through when your lives are charmed*
> *and a tragedy occurs.?*
> *Are you tested to see if you can survive?''*

Unable to find an answer, you may be angry - at everyone from your partner to your children to the doctor and even God. The least little statement from a friend may set you off in a fury.

> *I was very angry with everyone including God. When I see a dope head*
> *on TV or on the street I still think, why my son? I can hardly stand to see*
> *a gun of any kind or be around people who are drinking alcohol heavily.*

You also may **cry** frequently, although this is a very individual response. Some people cannot cry, while others cannot do so in public. Crying often comes in waves and can reflect anger, frustration, despair, helplessness, shame, guilt or even relief.

Sometimes parents feel guilty that they survived and their child did not. Siblings, too, can feel guilty that they lived and their brother or sister did not. Guilt can lead to feelings of shame and self-blame in both children and adults. **Guilt is a normal part of grief!**

I kept asking, "Why my child? Why Jason?"
What have I done to cause him to die?
What could I have done to prevent his death?

You also may fear death and be over-sensitive at first.
You may still deny the death, finding it impossible to believe.
Each little reminder is a challenge to your denial.

There are a lot of events that keep you busy but you're very conscious of the time and that this person will not be talking to you again or will not be hugging you or kissing you or calling you.
It really brings the reality to all of us. How very, very temporary life is.

You also may be dreaming about your child- -at night when you are asleep or during the day- -and you may have a sense that she is there with you.

For a long time after my son died, I went into his room,
just to touch his blanket, his toys.
I would be overwhelmed with pain, but it was something I just had to do.
It was the way I felt he was with me.

My dreams turned into nightmares nearly every night.
I would awaken screaming and it was always the same- -
a man standing over me with a gun.

During this time of physical and emotional exhaustion, you may find yourself pulling away from others to conserve your strength and energy. During this phase you may have difficulty sleeping, yet rest and sleep are important. It is wise to avoid alcohol and/or drugs.

Conservation \ Withdrawal

Just when you thought you would be feeling better, the black cloud seems bigger and darker. This may be the most frightening time of all because all you want to do is to be alone. You may not want to even get out of bed. You may feel like you are losing your mind.

This was the worst time for me. I thought I should be better, but I wasn't.
I couldn't eat. I couldn't sleep yet I didn't want to get out of bed.
All I wanted was for the world to go away.

One reason you withdraw is that your body needs to conserve energy. You hibernate to allow your body to rest, regain comfort and strength.

Your need to rest and withdraw gives your mind and body the strength to come to grips with the painful reality that all of the tears, yearning and searching have not brought your child back. This is the time when you despair because your life with your child is over forever.

Worse yet, you may have very little support during this time. Your family and friends have gone on with their lives and do not realize that you are still grieving. They believe you have picked up the pieces and moved on with life. This may be a time of great helplessness, particularly if your life revolved around your child.

I tried to go to the high school ball games but would just end up crying.
I am not ready to go yet. I still do not go.
My husband goes alone.

This also may be a time when you and your partner are unhappy with each other. The reason may be that you are grieving differently. Encourage each other to be open about feeling and accept each other's differences. It may seem very difficult, but this acceptance can ultimately make your relationship stronger and you can become more committed as a couple.

I really believe you are on a seesaw with your partner during this time.
When one of you is up, the other is down.
It's not that you don't care about how she feels.
When you are up you get frustrated if you can't bring your partner up.

During this time you may feel weakness, fatigue, and a need for more sleep. Because your body's ability to fight off disease will be weakened, you may be susceptible to more infectious diseases, such as colds and other viruses. It's a time when you need to take good care of yourself, even if it seems like a tremendous effort.

This phase can also be a time when you increase activities with the hope that by doing something useful, you'll feel better sooner. Be careful. Overdoing activities can increase your fatigue.

You may also find yourself going over the events of the death repeatedly in your mind, as well as your memories of your child. These thoughts and preoccupations with your memories are part of grieving.

I can be anywhere, at any time, even alone, when I get the feeling of almost a flashback phenomena where I can recall scenes at the hospital, the whole event of the funeral, and so on. I still can push it back when I want to, but it surprises me when it comes to the forefront.

It is from this concentration that ultimately you will be able to reach a turning point. This process may be slow or fast, but ultimately you will decide whether or not you will continue your life without your child. You will decide whether you will pick up the pieces and cope, or be forever locked in as a woman or man defined only as a *grieving parent*. This can be a conscious decision. In effect, it is a decision about whether you will be a survivor. It does not come overnight, a month or a year. It comes when you are ready.

Now that I think back it really was traumatic, but I was a tough old cookie!

Even when you feel terrible, when you rightfully feel sorry for yourself, remember - *the best way to honor your dead child is to take care of yourself.* Your child would not want it any other way. Your child would certainly not want to feel responsible for prolonged grieving.

Healing

It will seem as if you will never smile again, but you will. You will change the way you look at yourself from being a grieving parent to one who has lost a child but has moved on and survived. To get here, you accept the loss in your mind and heart and make changes in your life accordingly.

I can't tell you when the moment came, but it was like we decided as a family that we would not be destroyed by our son's death.
We would be survivors.
It may seem odd to say it, but I felt proud that we had made that decision on some unconscious level.

If it doesn't kill you, it will make you stronger.
But what a struggle it is.
I have decided to be a survivor.
It feels good to laugh once more."

During this time, you begin to take control over your life and make decisions about the future. This occurs slowly, over time. Men often feel they need better control over their emotions, while women seek control over their home, work and family life.

One of the difficulties about losing a child is a loss of roles. Not only are you no longer mother or father to this child, you have lost any group to which the child belonged. This child can no longer help you shop or fix the car. Now, as a way of letting go, you take on new roles and activities.

During this time, you likely have physical healing. You have less physical pain. You have more energy and are sleeping better. You may also start forgiving yourself for surviving and not being able to prevent your child's death. You will be able to let go - never forgetting your child, but letting go of the pain.

This is also a time when you may search for meaning for the loss. You may wonder what the death meant and how your son or daughter will be remembered. You may look for a way to help others in a similar situation. You find new friends and begin to find things to look forward to. This is a turning point. You are becoming a survivor.

How do I think I'm doing? Oh, I think I'm pretty good. I really do. In fact, I marvel at it all...to be able to get up and put my shoes on and get out there in the world and try and do the very best that I can knowing that I am going through a very, very hard and sad time.
Every so often I find myself laughing, and that feels good.

Renewal

The day will come when you will feel **normal** again. This will be a *new* normal. You will never be exactly the same as you were before. The scars will remain forever. With renewal comes new levels of functioning, a new awareness of yourself. You are probably stronger and have more energy.

You will have learned something important about yourself and your ability to cope. Grief teaches us much more about ourselves than does happiness. You have discovered more courage and stability than you ever thought possible.

I won't pretend to understand, but it certainly made us all more compas-
sionate and understanding of different lifestyles.
I kept a daily diary during his illness and I feel when I'm ready,
I'll read it ... not yet.

There is no reason to feel guilty about laughing or smiling again. You have earned the right to be happy just by having gone through the hard job of grieving.

I feel proud that we have patched up and have survived.
We have happiness in our lives- -a different happiness.
We will forever be sad to have lost Matt, but we did not let it destroy us.

Bittersweet Grief

You never forget your child, nor would you ever want to! Because of all your memories and life experiences, grief has a way of sneaking up on you. Birthdays, Christmas, Hanukkah, anniversaries of the death, expected date of graduation, Mother's Day, Father's Day and many day-to-day activities of life can trigger *re-grief.* This re-grief, sometimes called *bittersweet grief,* if a mixture of sadness and sweetness.

As soon as I get over one holiday, I'm looking at the next one. I'm not saying I should ignore those days, I just treat them differently so I don't have to whip myself by doing the same thing.

The days preceding her birthday were actually harder for me than her birthday itself. Not knowing how I would feel made the days before harder than the day itself. On her birthday, some high school friends invited me to the cemetery with them and I listened as they shared their thoughts about her. This was very special for me.

There are some things you can do to help you through special days.

*Recognize the day and spend time remembering.
*Bake a birthday cake, have your child's favorite meal.
*Fill your child's Christmas stocking with fresh flowers.
*Do something entirely different.
*Dedicate the day to your child - visit a nuring home, volunteer in honor of your daughter or son.
*Decorate the grave for holidays.
*Change holiday rituals such as opening presents at a new time.
*Plan your days instead of letting things happen.
*Plant enjoyable times: going to the movies, to the zoo, out for dinner, taking a short trip.

You can expect to experience bittersweet grief throughout your life, although it will not be as intense or last as long. Some sadness will forever be in your heart even after you have returned to a *new normal* life.

Men and Women and Grief

Grieving is very personal. No two people--even if you have been married for a long time--grieve the same way. In a marriage, differences in grieving can be especially hard to understand. After all, you were both the child's parents. Why don't you cry at the same time or feel angry at the same time? Why is she able to laugh? How can he go out with friends?

I just don't understand it. We were both Katie's parents, but he doesn't seem to be bothered that she died. Sure, he was sad in the beginning. Now, he just goes off to work and never wants to talk about it.

Working is my only relief from thinking, thinking, thinking. When I'm at work, I don't have time to feel sad. It hurts too much to talk about Katie. When my wife starts to talk about her, I just want to run away. I don't want to break down. After all, men aren't supposed to do that. We're supposed to be tough.

Both of you are hurting. You are just showing it in different ways. Men frequently--but not always--bury themselves in their work. They often do not want to talk because they are afraid of breaking out in tears. While our society is changing, many men still believe crying is a sign of weakness. They are conditioned to think, "Big boys don't cry," and that they are supposed to be the strong ones, the protectors.

Women, on the other hand, may sit and cry and want to talk repeatedly about their child. They may spend days in tears. Women are encouraged to talk and generally have more friends willing to listen.

It is common for men to be asked about their wives after a death but not about themselves. Men are thought to be "holding up well," or "handling things," if they show no sign of pain.

You and your spouse may even alternate grieving. Sometimes women grieve the first year and men the next. Sometimes a mother will have a down day or week and feel better the next. Then Dad has his time.

Because men and women grieve differently, it's hard to understand each other. Just when you need to be pulling together, you pull apart. This can strain and stress a marriage.

We decided early on that we would not blame each other and that we would give each other space and time. It was a conscious decision and it wasn't always easy.

There are no simple ways to solve this problem. Maybe the best way is to be open with each other and accept your differences.

People usually deal with loss in one of three ways:

1. Put it behind you and move on. It's not that you forget about your loss, you just don't talk about it.

2. Get busy and fill the empty space. You may overwork, overeat, overdrink or get over-involved in support organizations trying to help.

3. Stay connected with your child. You remember your child at special times. You say, "Not a day goes by when I don't think of him."

Probably, you will use all three of these at one time or another. They are tools that help you survive. However, there are certain **red flags** which may indicate trouble in your marriage:

> Your partner's over-involvement in work, church, a support group or family
> Increased use of alcohol or drugs by either you or your partner
> Weight gain or loss of 15 pounds
> Persistent lack of sex and loving
> Talking constantly but never getting anything settled
> Separation or estrangement

If you feel you need help, get it. Seeking assistance is not a sign of weakness, it is an act of love- -to yourself and your family.

> And remember, keep on courting - even now.
> Talk about how you met and fell in love.
> Say what you love about each other.
> Go out on dates, even if it's just a walk in a park.

We did two things that saved us.
We agreed to have a two-minute hug every day.
At the end of the day, we asked each other, "How Are You?"
That way we touched comfortably, both physically and emotionally.

Grandparents Grieve, Too

There are other people in your life hurting over the loss of your child; your own parents. They hurt for the loss of their grandchild, and they are in anguish watching you suffer. Some grandparents say they have a double loss.

I guess you can say I really pushed the kids into having kids.
In my mind I thought about taking my grandson fishing and to ball games.
Now that he's gone, there's a hole in my life, too.

As a grandparent of a 3-month old SIDS victim, I am experiencing three devastating sorrows. I suffer the loss of a precious grandchild; I suffer because of my daughter's pain; and I mourn my daughter's loss of faith. She rejects a God who would allow this monstrous, unexplainable death.

You also may be in so much pain that you cannot see the pain your own parents are feeling. You may be unable to comfort them. You may even feel burdened by seeing them grieve.

I would look at my mother and know her heart was broken.

There can be other problems, too. If there are two sets of grandparents, you may be torn between families. Sometimes grandparents feel guilty, blaming themselves for surviving or passing on genes that may have caused the death. They may try to make things easier for you by making funeral arrangements and deciding things for you. They want to make it all better again, to take you on their laps and cuddle you and instead, they just add stress. Almost always they mean well and they do what they do out of love.

Long-distance relationships are also difficult. Not only are grandparents not there to give hugs, a telephone call or letter can be misunderstood.

I dreaded calls from my mother. I knew she meant well and loved our son as much as we did. I just couldn't stand her pain on top of mine. It was just too much. When she called, I just felt myself turning cold and angry.

You are grieving. Your emotions are unstable. Grandparents can be easy targets for your anger and your hurt because they have always accepted you before and still will. Just as you need to be sensitive to their pain, so must they accept your need to work through your grief in your own way. Grandparents can be sources for support and strength. Having lived their own lives they likely have survived their own struggles.

I can give her my love and my prayers and my care and my concern.
I could give her my life, but that won't help.

I am powerlessness. I am helplessness. I am frustration. I sit with her and I cry with her. She cries for her daughter and I cry for mine. I can't help her. I can't reach inside her and take her broken heart. I must watch her suffer day after day.

I listen to her tell me over and over how she misses Emily, how she wants her back. I can't bring Emily back for her. I can't buy her an even better Emily than she had, like I could buy her and even better toy when she was a child. I can't kiss the hurt and make it go away. I can't even kiss a small part of it away. There's no bandaid large enough to cover her bleeding heart.

There was a time I could listen to her talk about a fickle boyfriend and tell her it would be okay, and know in my heart that in two weeks she wouldn't even think of him. Can I tell her it'll be okay in two years when I know it will never be okay, that she will carry this pain of "what might have been" in her deepest heart for the rest of her life?

I see this young woman, my child, who was once carefree and fun-loving and bubbling with life, slumped in a chair with her eyes full of agony. Where is my power now? Where is my mother's bag of tricks that will make it all better?

Why can't I join her in the aloneness of her grief? As tight as my arms wrap around her, I can't reach that aloneness.

What can I give her to make her better? A cold, wet cloth will ease the swelling of her crying eyes, but it won't stop the reason for her tears. What treat will bring joy back to her? What prize will bring that happy child smile back? Where are the magic words to give her comfort? What chapter in Dr. Spock tells me how to do this? He has told me everything else I've needed to know.

> *Where are the answers?*
> *I should have them.*
> *I'm the mother.*

I know that someday she'll find happiness again, that her life will have meaning again. I can hold out hope for her someday, but what about now? this minute? this hour? this day?

I can give her my love and my prayers and my care and my concern. I could give her my life. But even that won't help.

From: *For Bereaved Grandparents*
by Margaret Gerner

Your Other Children

Your other children may not be able to put their feelings into words. Some may be too young to understand what death means, but they will all be aware of a loss in your home. They see you and many others upset and know something unusual is going on.

Children and the funeral. How involved your children should be in the funeral depends on your own experiences with death, your values, their age, maturity and their wishes. But children do surprisingly well, particularly if they are prepared for what they will see. Letting them attend the funeral gives them memories for future discussions. It indicates an openness. It lets them know that you will include them in important family times, and this is one of the most important things a family will ever do together. One mother simply told her children that families that play together and work together and laugh together grieve together, too.

I always thought children had to be protected from funerals and death. But when their brother or sister dies, they are a part of it. They can accept much more than I thought.

Children may want to be involved in many different ways. For a young child, picking out a grave may be comforting. A teenager or adult child may want to be involved in more ways.

When they went to put the makeup on my daughter at the funeral home, my other daughter said, "I brought her makeup and I'll do it" She simply put the make-up on just like she always wore it. My husband said, "What a special thing to do--the ultimate good deed for your sister."

Grief: Children grieve, going through all the grief emotions. Usually, their grief seems to be short-lived, but it exists and returns every so often. Sometimes children need to do something for their sibling, something that gives finality or creates a special memory of that brother or sister.

When our son's birthday came, his sister (age 6) wanted to celebrate. She asked if we could push the table over against the window, just like at his funeral. Her memory of that funeral was of the table full of food surrounded by a festive crowd. When we have a party, she still wants to push the table over against the window. It's a bittersweet memory that I've grown to treasure.

Our son didn't say much, but I did see him slip a penny in Jessica's casket. I think it was something he wanted to give her.

You may see your children with a wide range of responses, including:

---- Acting out	---- Loss of appetite
---- Anxiety attacks	---- Nightmares
---- Acting grown up	---- Sadness
---- Bed wetting	---- Separation anxiety
---- Crying	---- Stuttering
---- Depression	---- Suicide attempts
---- Talking about the dead child	---- Difficulty in school
---- Health problems	---- Aggressiveness
---- Irritability	---- Withdrawn behaviors

If these last for some time, children may need professional help. Getting help is not a sign of failure or that you are not a good parent. It says you love your children and you care.

Our oldest son really had a struggle.
He had such a special relationship with his youngest brother.
He has had some therapy and is doing better.

Understanding death. How well children understand what has happened depends on their age and the way you handle it.

When our daughter died, our other daughter was 8.
When I asked her if she ever thought about her sister, her answer was,
"It makes me too sad so I try not to think about her."
Her room was beside her sister's so for a time after her death she slept
with us in our bed, then moved to a blow-up mattress in our room and
finally back to her own bed in her own room.

It's important to be honest. Tell children their sister or brother is *dead.* If a child asks, "What is dead?" you may want to say that the body stops working. Explain that death is not like sleep where all your body parts are working away, doing their job. Talk about other times when a pet has died or when the leaves fall in Autumn. Explain that while the child will hear people say words like, "lost" or "sleeping" that's not what dead means. Share your beliefs, and at the same time, be careful about telling a child her sibling is with God. It's easy for children to picture God as a child-snatcher or think their brother went to be with God because they were bad. Be sure they know nothing they did or thought caused the death.

Edna St Vincent Millay described childhood as *the kingdom where nobody dies.* This is a fantasy of adults where we can make our children live forever. Sharing the truth about death may be uncomfortable, but it is the most helpful way to talk to our children.

Before age 5, children are most often afraid of being abandoned. They believe death to be temporary and not final. Games of peek-a-boo and hide and seek say people go away and then come back.

Between 5 and 9, children think of death as an angel or a ghost. Death is something that happens to other things and old people.

After age 10, children come to realize death is final and that it happens to everyone. But, like all of us, they have strong denials and hope to put it off as long as possible.

The most difficult moment for us was when they began lowering my son's casket into the grave. Until this time it had been almost like a lark to Maggie, all these people over all the time. But when the casket started going down, she was startled and asked, "How will we get him back"

Some children ask many questions about death. Others close up and will not talk at all. Some children are so open they chatter on about their loss with strangers.

We were at the grocery story when my son said, "My sister died."'' I felt my face grow hot, tears well in my eyes, yet I smiled, too.

Sometimes, questions from children come out of nowhere. They are unexpected and you may be caught off guard. As children get older they tend to ask questions again from a new perspective.

Guilt. Children can feel guilty because they are living and their brother or sister is not. Young children are often *magical* thinkers. They may think their thoughts killed their brother or sister. They need to be told that wishing to be an only child or wishing their sibling dead, did not make it happen. They need to know that you love them as individuals and that it is OK for them to be alive.

I never wanted my daughter to donate her bone marrow because I didn't want her to feel guilty if her brother died. But it was our only option. About six months after he died, she told me her bone marrow wasn't good enough. I hugged her and told her that she had made a great gift to him. She needed to hear that several times over the next year.

Children's feelings often come out in dreams and play.

It was interesting to watch my children play doctor.
My daughter always played "ear checks"
while my son always played bone marrow biopsy or I.V.
I knew when he died, that we would have some interesting games
ahead. She played funeral with her dolls - the parents always cried.
Later, when she began writing short stories in school,
her characters frequently died, often from leukemia.

Perfecting. One problem children face is that people often glorify the dead child, making her perfect..It is impossible to live up to that image.

We realized that we were making him into an angel.
All we talked about was Ronnie this and Ronnie that.
When Craig apologized for not being perfect, we really felt bad.

Comforters. Children often find themselves in the role of having to be comforters to their parents, a role many are much too young to handle. They hold their feelings in because they do not want to add to your pain.

We realized she was taking care of us.
She wouldn't talk about Jess because every time she did, we cried.

Uniqueness. Children may feel having a sibling die makes them different and they may be uncomfortable with that.

My daughter came home from kindergarten and said, "
I'm the only kid in class whose brother died."'
"I know," I told her.
"I'm the only mother whose son has died. We're in this together."

Take time! Many families have found it helpful to have special times with their surviving children. By giving them additional attention as special people, it keeps the doors open for communication and makes them feel good.

Robert Cavanaugh, who wrote one of the early books on death and dying speaks of children dealing with grief. *Volkswagens do the same job as Cadallacs,* he says. Given love and support and honest answers, children handle grief as well as and sometimes better than we adults do.

Friends and Family

The death of a child causes so much pain that few people, even those who have gone through it, know what to say or do to help and show they care. At first many, many people rush in with a casserole or food. They gather around you, telling you they are sorry and trying to help.

We had food in the dining room and people all over the house.
It really helped. It would be hard to come home to an empty house.
It is really nice to have people who talked about her and remembered her.

Well-meaning people frequently put their feet in their mouths, however, making statements that unintentionally hurt.

Someone said, "One good thing is you've lost a few pounds."
I was irate to think that's good news after such a catastrophe.

Family and friends so dearly want to do something--anything to take away your pain--that they sometimes go beyond their bounds. They may take charge, thinking you need it, and do such things as clean out your child's room. At the time, you may be in shock or unable to stand up against such seemingly positive help.

When my son died I had a friend who stepped in and did everything.
We really needed the help, or at least thought we did.
One day I suddenly was mad.
This was my child and it seemed like she had taken over.

Sometimes people stop mentioning your child, thinking the mention of her name will cause you pain. They try to give you an answer or reason for the death or a way to make it more acceptable, such as, 'She is with God now' or 'It was for the best.' Sometimes people simply suggest, 'you can have another one,' as if one child is interchangeable with another.

People say things that sound mean because they have had little experience with death. Death makes us feel uncomfortable, particularly the death of a child. We like to keep bad things at arm's length because we do not like to think about losing our own children or dying ourselves. It is reality, too, that some people are just better at expressing themselves than others.

Sometimes you must be a teacher while you are grieving. You have to let people know what will help you. You have to show them that it is OK for you- - and for them- -to cry, that you need them to be with you, to listen and accept what you say. You need them to understand your child may have died, but he remains an important part of your life in your heart.

I could sense people freezing if I brought up my son's name.
As they watched me tell stories about him, just as I do my other children,
they became used to the idea that it was OK to talk about him.
Even if my eyes fill up with tears, they realize it is OK.
Today, the greatest gift they can give me is to remember him.

Remember the intentions of family and friends as being good, even if the words sometimes come out wrong. You may need to tell people at times that something they said hurt you. Do so gently, saying something like: *That's not how I see it, I don't feel that way,* or *What you are saying hurts me.*

If you do not feel up to talking about it so directly, just say, *Thank you for your support,* or *Thank you for thinking of us.*

As time goes on, family and friends will go on with their lives. It is not that they have forgotten you, it is just that they have moved on and assume you have as well. If you need help, support or a sensitive ear, ask for it. You will find friends and family want to help, but just need to know from you what would help you.

His classmates held a car wash to help with expenses.
They were so proud when I told them we used that money
for his helicopter ride to the medical center.

You may be overwhelmed about all the good that was done for you in your time of tragedy. It is impossible to thank all those who have helped you. Giving to others in need may be the best way to express your appreciation.

I said to my friend, "How can I ever repay you?"
She said, "I don't want you to.
Someone was good to me a while back.
I'm doing this for you and you'll help someone else."

Picking Up the Pieces

One of the problems of grief is knowing whether you are doing okay or are "normal." The question is whether your grief is healthy.

I was in so much pain I didn't know if I was crazy or not.
I would go to the store and spend twenty minutes
trying to decide between beans and peas.

No one expects you to forget your child or to go on as if your son or daughter has not died. After all, you have lost your child, a person who has been an extremely important part of your life in many ways.

Still, there are several ways you can tell how you are doing. Some people keep a record of their feelings from month to month to keep track of their progress.

You can ask yourself these questions:

- Am I taking care of myself?
    Do I pay attention to my hair, clothing and appearance?
- Am I taking care of my partner and other children?
    Am I meeting their emotional and physical needs?

- Am I able to take care of my home?
    Can I do housework, cooking, yardwork, maintenance?
- Am I allowing myself happiness or pleasure?
    Can I laugh without feeling guilty?
    Do I enjoy being out with friends and co-workers?
    Do I feel pleasure in sexual experiences?

- Is my world beyond myself?
    Can I sit quietly and think of things other than my child?
    Am I interested in events in the community and in the news?
- Can I talk about my child dying without tremendous sadness, anger, jealousy or guilt?

- Do I feel the black cloud over me has passed?
- Have I resumed my job, church work, volunteer work, clubs, sports teams- -the things I did and enjoyed before my child died?

- Do I notice the beauty in the world again- -the things I enjoyed, like favorite foods, places, and events?
- Can I sleep again and get up feeling refreshed?

- Can I concentrate on work and take part in conversations?
- Can I think more clearly and am I less forgetful?
- Can I recall events in the past?

-Do I feel more in control, better able to cope with what others say or do and with day-to-day life?
- Do I feel less frantic, panicked or worried?

- Can I think that something good came out of the loss, such as new knowledge of my own strengths and ability to cope?
- Am I able to make decisions?

There is no right or wrong number of yes or no answers to these questions. As time goes on, you will find you can answer yes more often. For some of us, there will be "no's" even when we are *not* grieving!

There are some *red flags* in grief. If you spot these in yourself, your partner or your children - **get help!**

*Constant thoughts of suicide, especially if you are developing a plan
* Isolating yourself from others
* Gaining or losing a lot of weight
    15 pounds of your body weight
* Increasing your use of alcohol, nicotine or other drugs
* Being persistently unable to sleep
* Being unable to care for the needs of your surviving children
* Being unable to care for yourself
* Throwing yourself into your work excessively
* Spending increasing periods of time away from home
* Throwing yourself into religion
    to the point of excluding other parts of your life
* Blaming others for the loss or for other troubles
* Hostile feelings toward your partner, children or other family
    members and friends.

Everyone feels hostile, blames others and has off days now and then. However, if you see yourself a lot in the above list, you're seeing red flags. Get help. Sometimes it helps to talk to a professional for reassurance that what you are feeling is normal and to be reminded that grieving takes time.

Among sources for help are a medical social worker you may have met in the hospital, a counselor of the American Association of Marriage and Family Practitioners, or a representative of the Association for Death Education and Counseling. Your yellow pages list several people and agencies to whom you can turn. If you try a counselor and you feel you're not making progress or that it's not a right fit, try another.

Helping Yourself

While there is no magical way through the grieving process, there are ways that you can help yourself. In a sense, they help you to stay healthy so that you can deal with the pain you are feeling.

Talk with your partner, family and friends about your child and how you feel. When you do this, you release bottled-up emotions and tensions. You also set an example for others so they know it is all right to still consider your child an important part of your life.

Keep in touch. Try to resume old relationships and start new ones as a couple and as individuals. Your old friends have a history with your child, but new friends offer new opportunities. Old school friends who have a history with you may want to listen and offer support.

Take care of your body. Take special care with your diet to make sure it includes the nutrients your body needs under stress. Make sure you include milk, meat, vegetables, fruit and whole grains and avoid junk foods and fast foods that supply empty calories. If you can afford frozen meals, look for ones that are more nutritionally sound- -low in fat, sugar and salt. Take a multi-vitamin every day.

Drink water. At least eight glasses of liquids a day are needed to keep you hydrated and to wash away body wastes. You may want to place a pitcher or jug of water in the refrigerator for cold drinks all day.

Avoid alcohol, caffeine and tobacco. They can cause dehydration, headaches and/or low back pain. Alcohol drains your body of vitamins, increases the acidity of your stomach, decreases your circulation and can cause heart palpitations (fluttering). It can also make you feel more sad.

Exercise or do something active every day- -walking, biking, jogging, aerobics or stretching. Exercise helps you physically and psychologically. Getting outside and moving, even if it is just a walk around the block, can be refreshing and reduce stress. Kelly Osmont, in her book, *More Than Surviving,* tells about not feeling like walking. She listed all the excuses she could, then imagined them being swished away with windshield wipers.

Rest. With the stress on your body, you need rest even if you cannot sleep. This is not the time to increase your work hours. If you cannot sleep at night, try sleeping with a special article of clothing, such as a stuffed toy or a blanket of your child's. Warm milk before bedtime, listening to relaxation tapes or writing in your journal, can also be helpful.

Keep a journal, write letters, notes, poems, or record your feelings on tape. Doing this can help release emotions.

Read - books, articles and poems. Reading can help you understand what has happened and lets you know that you are not alone. Your local librarian and bookstores can help you find good material.

Admit when you need help. If you are not comfortable with the way you are getting along in your grief, seek help. Roughly 40 percent of people who lose a child go for counseling of one kind or another to lessen their pain and loneliness.

Accept help from others. You do not have to do it all alone. There are many people who want to help you by providing food, keeping you company, doing housework and helping out with your other children. Call the people who wrote you a note with their sympathy cards, saying, ''Let me know if I can be of any help.'' Take them up on their offers.

If you need to *cry,* rent a sad movie. It helps you let out your feelings.

Talk to a clergyperson you trust if you need help regaining your faith and hope.

Attend a self-help or support group. Your clinic or hospital will know about support groups for parents who have lost a child. You'll find other people who have gone through a similar loss will be able to give you support, help and hope in a way that others cannot. They really **do** know how you feel.

Reach out to someone else in pain.

It is in giving that we receive.
It is in wishing to let our hearts break again,
that we allow our hearts to heal and not turn to stone.

Don't worry about how someone else might respond to a loss of a child or what others might think. You are responsible for your feelings not someone else's.

Every family has its own definition of normal.
We had our own style of normal when our daughter was with us
and we have a different style of normal without her.
I can't tell people enough not to worry
about how someone else handled a death. Do what is right for you.

Re-entering Life

After the death of your child, you will find you have may *firsts*. Some are obvious- -the first birthday after the death, the first Christmas, the first anniversary of the death. Some firsts are less obvious- - the first day back to work, church, the store, etc. Many people in these places know you and you may be overwhelmed by their asking how you are doing.

There are bound to be uncomfortable moments. You will probably be anxious about how people will react. People will want to give you a hug, to make you feel welcome and to include you again in the activities. Others will dart away from you, embarrassed and uneasy. However, you will discover caring people wherever you go.

There will be insensitive people. Even well-meaning friends and co-workers may occasionally say the wrong thing. Again, it helps to listen to the intention, not just the particular words.

While you will never go back to the *normal* you had in your life before your child's death, there is hope. Most people eventually go on with their lives-- at their own pace and on their own timetables.

She absorbed and reflected a point of my soul
and when she died a part of me died, too.
It has taken me years to come back, but I am now growing again.

The hurt doesn't go away, it just doesn't come as often. You learn to honor your child by taking care of yourself. Your child would want the best for you. One poster said simply, *When you are depressed, close your eyes and ask your dead child what to do.*

You learn to value your memories, to laugh again. You learn to walk tall and reach out to others. You learn that you can survive.

Someone said, "Pain is a part of life, but misery is an option."
At the time I didn't know the difference and plummeted into the depths.
I got on with life but with indifference.
Now I'm living each day completely and my daughter is a loving memory.

Margaret M. Pike, RN, EdD, has a doctorate in education and has worked in health care administration, been a university faculty member and has co-authored books for bereavement support groups. She has co-facilitated numerous support groups for grieving people. Margie lives in Nineveh, Indiana with her husband, Frank. Siobhan, her daughter, is grown and married.

Sara Wheeler, RN, MSN co-created the national Resolve Through Sharing Program for people dealing with miscarriage, stillbirth and neonatal loss. She is Associate Professor at Lakeview College of Nursing and is studying for her doctorate in Psychiatric/Mental Health. Sara and Gary have two children, Nate and Lori, and live in Covington, Indiana.

Both Sara and Margie are founders of *Grief Ltd.,*
an organization dedicated to making a difference in people's lives.